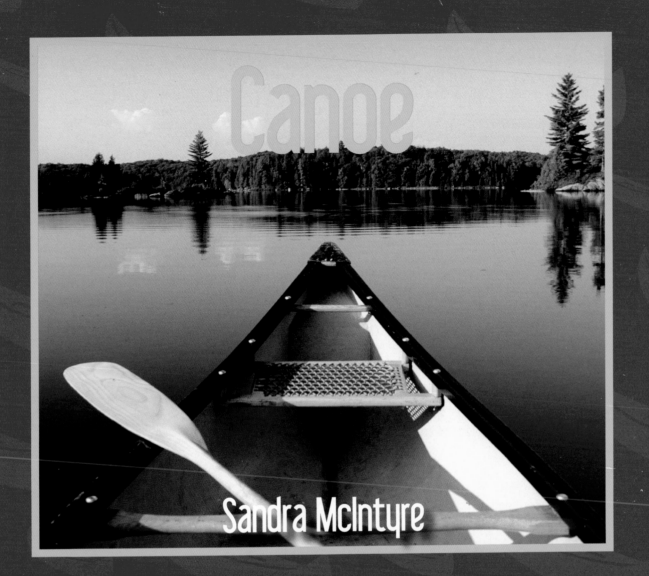

Canoe

Sandra McIntyre

Weigl

Published by Weigl Educational Publishers Limited
6325 10th Street SE
Calgary, Alberta T2H 2Z9
Website: www.weigl.com

Library and Archives Canada Cataloguing in Publication

McIntyre, Sandra, 1970-
          Canoes : Canadian icons / Sandra McIntyre.
Includes index.
Also available in electronic format.
ISBN 978-1-77071-575-2 (bound).--ISBN 978-1-77071-582-0 (pbk.)

          1. Canoes and canoeing--Canada--Juvenile literature. 2. Indians of North
America--Boats--Canada--Juvenile literature. I. Title.

E98.B6M35 2010   j623.82'9   C2010-903741-3

Printed in the United States of America in North Mankato, Minnesota
1 2 3 4 5 6 7 8 9 0 14 13 12 11 10

072010
WEP230610

Editor: Heather Kissock
Design: Terry Paulhus

Weigl acknowledges Getty Images and Alamy as image suppliers for this title.

We acknowledge the financial support of the Government of Canada through the Canada Book Fund for our
publishing activities.

CONTENTS

What is a Canoe?

A canoe is a lightweight, narrow boat. Canoes usually hold one or two people. Canoeing is a popular **pastime** and sport in Canada. People can paddle around lakes or race down rivers in a canoe. Canoes are often used for fishing.

Canoe History

Long ago, **First Nations** used canoes for hunting and travelling. European **fur traders** began using canoes when they came to Canada. The traders travelled by water to forests. There, they would collect animal furs. Sometimes, the traders used large canoes. These canoes could carry 12 people and more than 3,600 kilograms of supplies. The men who paddled these canoes were called voyageurs.

Canoe Size

Today, most canoes are about 4.5 metres long. They can be as short as 3 metres or as long as 6.1 metres. A long canoe can carry more weight. It is also easier to steer. A short canoe is light. It is good for making quick twists and turns.

Ocean liner: Up to 345 metres

Compare Boat Lengths

Kayak: Up to 3 metres

Canoe: About 4.5 metres

Tugboat: Up to 22.5 metres

What is a Canoe Made of?

The first canoes were made of tree trunks that were hollowed out. Later, Canada's First Nations used wood and tree **bark** to build canoes. They often used birchbark. Birchbark is waterproof and strong. Today, most canoes are made from wood or **canvas**.

The Parts of a Canoe

All canoes have the same basic shape. Most canoes are open. This means they do not have a cover. Some canoes have seats for sitting or kneeling. Each part of a canoe has a word to describe it. The same words are also used to describe other kinds of boats.

BOW The front of the canoe is called the bow.

GUNWALES The top of the canoe's sides are called gunwales.

HULL The outside of the canoe is called the hull.

STERN The back end of the canoe is called the stern.

Paddling Basics

A paddle is the tool used to make a canoe move. A paddle has three main parts. The grip is the handle on top of the paddle. It does not touch the water. The shaft is the long arm of the paddle. The blade is at the end of the paddle. It is the part that goes in the water.

The paddle is held with both hands and pulled through the water. This action is called a stroke. Each stroke moves the canoe forward.

Carrying a Canoe

Many lakes and rivers stretch across Canada. Not all lakes and rivers are connected, however. Sometimes, a canoe must be taken out of the water and carried to the next body of water. The act of carrying a canoe is called *portage*. This is a French word that means "carry."

The Places You Will Go

There are two basic kinds of canoeing. Some people prefer to have a quiet journey on a calm lake. Flatwater canoeing is most often done on calm waters. Others prefer an active ride. Whitewater canoeing is done on fast-moving, choppy waters.

A Day at the Races

Canoe racing is an Olympic sport. The races in the Olympics are called sprints. These races range from 200 to 1,000 metres in length.

Another type of canoe race is the marathon. These are much longer races. The longest canoe marathon in the world is the Yukon 1000. People paddle their canoes 1,600 kilometres down the Yukon River.

Make a Paper Canoe

Supplies

Construction
paper

crayons

scissors

yarn

a hole punch

1. Fold the piece of paper in half lengthwise.

2. Make another fold about a 1.5 centimetres from the first fold line. Repeat on the other side of the original fold. The paper should now look like a "W." The folds will be the bottom of the canoe.

3. Draw a canoe shape on the paper, making sure the folds are on the bottom of the canoe.

4. Cut out the canoe shape, and punch a few holes on each end.

5. Weave the yarn through the holes.

6. Push the folded floor flat so that the canoe sits upright.

Find Out More

To learn more about canoes, visit a local canoe club or these websites.

All About Canoes
www.canoe.ca/
AllAboutCanoes

The Canoe Museum
www.canoe
museum.ca

**Hudson's Bay
Company History**
www.hbc.com/hbcheritage/
history/transportation/canoe

Canadian Canoe Association:
www.canoekayak.ca

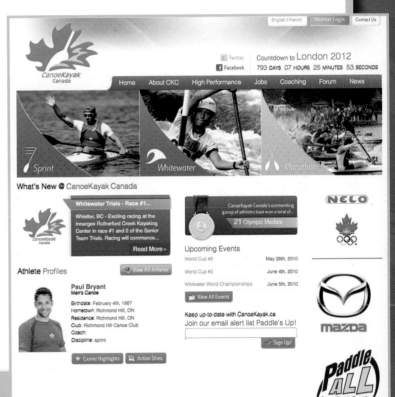

Glossary

bark: the outside of a tree

canvas: a heavy fabric

First Nations: the original inhabitants of Canada

fur traders: people who obtain animal furs and trade them for money or other items

pastime: an activity done when a person has spare time

Index